THE HUMAN BODY

# THE NERVOUS SYSTEM

By Heather Moore Niver

**Gareth Stevens**
Publishing

**Please visit our website, www.garethstevens.com. For a free color catalog of all our high-quality books, call toll free 1-800-542-2595 or fax 1-877-542-2596.**

**Library of Congress Cataloging-in-Publication Data**

Niver, Heather Moore.
The nervous system / Heather Moore Niver.
    p. cm. — (The human body)
Includes index.
ISBN 978-1-4339-6590-6 (pbk.)
ISBN 978-1-4339-6591-3 (6-pack)
ISBN 978-1-4339-6588-3 (library binding)
1.  Nervous system—Juvenile literature.  I. Title.
QP361.5.N58 2012
612.8'1—dc23

                                          2011031187

First Edition

Published in 2012 by
**Gareth Stevens Publishing**
111 East 14th Street, Suite 349
New York, NY 10003

Copyright © 2012 Gareth Stevens Publishing

Designer: Daniel Hosek
Editor: Greg Roza

Photo credits: Cover, p. 1 Ingram Publishing/The Agency Collection/Getty Images; all backgrounds, pp. 4–5 (all images), 7 (all images), 9, 13 (all images), 15, 21, 23 (tick close-up), 25 (painter, sudoku), 27 (all images), 28–29 Shutterstock.com; p. 11 MedicalRF.com/Getty Images; p. 17 Pasieka/Science Photo Library/Getty Images; p. 19 Dorling Kindersley/Getty Images; p. 23 (tick on finger) iStockphoto.com; p. 25 (runners) Mark Herreid/Shutterstock.com.

Printed in the United States of America

CPSIA compliance information: Batch #CW12GS: For further information contact Gareth Stevens, New York, New York at 1-800-542-2595.

# Contents

Thinking About the Nervous System . . . 4

Supercomputer, Superhighway . . . . . . . 6

Running Automatically . . . . . . . . . . . . 8

Peripheral Nerves . . . . . . . . . . . . . . . . 10

Know Your Noggin . . . . . . . . . . . . . . 12

How It All Works . . . . . . . . . . . . . . . . 16

Your Changing Brain . . . . . . . . . . . . . 20

Diseases and Disorders . . . . . . . . . . . . 22

Keep Your Brain in Shape! . . . . . . . . . . 24

Other Animals' Nervous Systems . . . . . 26

Use Your Brain! . . . . . . . . . . . . . . . . . 28

Glossary . . . . . . . . . . . . . . . . . . . . . . . 30

For More Information . . . . . . . . . . . . . 31

Index . . . . . . . . . . . . . . . . . . . . . . . . . 32

Words in the glossary appear in **bold** type
the first time they are used in the text.

You feel the warm sun on your skin and taste cold chocolate ice cream on your tongue. This is your nervous system at work. You use your five senses—sight, hearing, touch, smell, and taste—constantly. They give you information about what's happening to you and around you. Information is speeding through your nervous system—which is made up of your brain, spinal cord, and **nerves**—all the time.

Whenever nerves send a message to the brain, your brain decides what to do and tells the body how to act. This happens when you pull back from something hot. You need your nervous system to do things such as read, eat, sleep, run, laugh, and even remember. You can't do much without your nervous system.

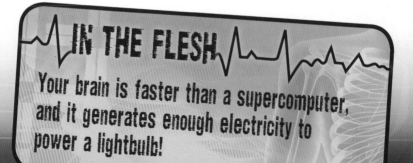

## IN THE FLESH

Your brain is faster than a supercomputer, and it generates enough electricity to power a lightbulb!

4

# HOT, HOT, HOT!

When you sip some steaming hot cocoa, you immediately stop drinking when your tongue feels the extreme heat. It doesn't seem to take any thought, but in that split second, a lot of activity is going on in your body. Nerves in your tongue send a message about pain up to your brain. Your brain immediately sends a message to your hand to pull the mug away. Burn avoided.

This X-ray of a human body shows the nervous system in red.

# Supercomputer, Superhighway

The brain and spinal cord make up the central nervous system. Your brain is kind of like your body's central computer. It's in charge of every single action and reaction you have. And it does this in almost no time at all.

Your spinal cord is like a highway along which messages speed to and from the brain. The spinal cord is a long rope of nerve tissue that runs from the base of your brain down through the spine. Along the way, various nerves branch out and extend throughout your entire body. These nerves make up the peripheral nervous system, which transmits messages between the central nervous system and the rest of the body.

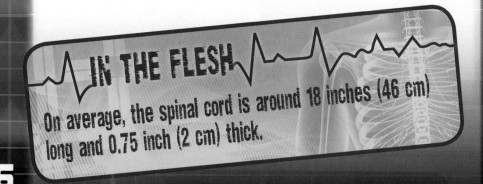

## IN THE FLESH

On average, the spinal cord is around 18 inches (46 cm) long and 0.75 inch (2 cm) thick.

The brain and spinal cord have a lot of important work to do. Of course, the body has some ways to protect them and make sure they stay healthy. Your skull protects your brain, and **vertebrae** are armor for the spinal cord. Layers of **membranes**, called meninges, and **cerebrospinal fluid** provide some padding. Cerebrospinal fluid also keeps the nerves healthy.

spinal cord

vertebrae

*This model shows how the spinal cord is surrounded and protected by vertebrae.*

7

# Automatically

So you have your central nervous system and your peripheral nervous system. But what part of your nervous system controls things like breathing, heartbeat, and emotions? Your peripheral nervous system has a part called the autonomic nervous system. This system regulates some body functions without you having to think about them.

The autonomic nervous system is divided into two major parts: sympathetic and parasympathetic. Sympathetic nerves prepare your body to react to an emergency, such as freezing cold conditions or an injury. They also kick in when your body's internal chemistry is out of balance. Parasympathetic nerves keep your body running when it's at rest. These two types of nerves sometimes work against each other, but they also balance one another out.

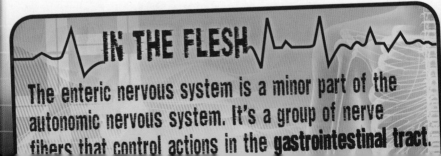

## IN THE FLESH

The enteric nervous system is a minor part of the autonomic nervous system. It's a group of nerve fibers that control actions in the **gastrointestinal tract**.

# FIGHT OR FLIGHT?

Sympathetic nerves help your body adjust to the world around you, such as when you sweat in hot weather. But when you face a threat or a difficult new challenge, the whole sympathetic nervous system kicks into high gear. Your lungs work harder and your heart pounds faster to send more oxygenated blood to your muscles. That way, you're ready to face the problem or quickly run for safety. This is called the "fight or flight" response.

# Peripheral Nerves

In the peripheral nervous system, there are two more groups of nerves besides autonomic. Spinal nerves originate in the spinal cord. They contain bunches of sensory and motor fibers, and humans have 31 pairs of them. Each connects the spinal cord to a certain part of the body. Motor fibers send information from the central nervous system to the muscles. Sensory fibers carry information from skin, muscles, joints, and internal organs to the spinal cord.

Cranial nerves join parts of the brain to sense organs in your head. They also connect to muscles, internal organs, and **glands** in the head and upper body. Cranial nerves are hard at work when you munch and then swallow a carrot. They also help you blink and make faces at your sister.

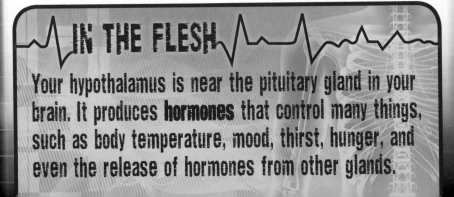

## IN THE FLESH

Your hypothalamus is near the pituitary gland in your brain. It produces **hormones** that control many things, such as body temperature, mood, thirst, hunger, and even the release of hormones from other glands.

This is a picture of the brainstem. Not shown here is the wrinkled outer layer of the brain normally shown.

# THE PITUITARY GLAND

At the base of your brain is a tiny gland called the pituitary (or hypophysis). Are your clothes getting too tight? You can thank your pituitary gland! It makes and releases special hormones to make your body grow. It's also responsible for releasing hormones that prompt puberty, which is the time when girls and boys develop into women and men. The pituitary also works with other glands to do things such as control the sugar and water in your body.

cranial nerve

pituitary gland

# Know Your Noggin

The brain is made up of three sections: the forebrain, midbrain, and hindbrain. The forebrain is the biggest and most complicated part. It's mainly made up of the cerebrum, which contains the information that gives each of us a personality—emotions, intelligence, and memory. It also allows us to feel and move around. Four areas of the cerebrum, called lobes, are responsible for different kinds of information storage and activities. The four lobes are called frontal, parietal, temporal, and occipital.

The cerebrum is divided into two halves, or hemispheres. The right half controls the left side of the body, and the left half is in charge of the right side of the body. A band between the two parts, called the corpus callosum, helps them communicate.

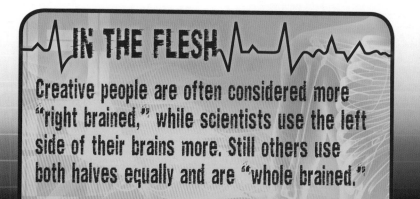

## IN THE FLESH

Creative people are often considered more "right brained," while scientists use the left side of their brains more. Still others use both halves equally and are "whole brained."

frontal lobe

parietal lobe

occipital lobe

temporal lobe

## TWO SIDES OF IT

The cerebrum's two hemispheres look a lot alike, but they do more than control different sides of the body. The right side of your brain is sensitive and creative. The left side is more logical and objective. So when you're grooving to your favorite music, the right side of your brain is in action. When you do your math homework, the left side is busy.

The outer layer of the cerebrum is called the cortex, or gray matter. It collects information from your five senses and then sends that information out to other parts of the nervous system. The thalamus, hypothalamus, and pituitary gland make up the inner part of the forebrain. The thalamus receives information from our sensory organs and passes it along to other parts of the brain. The hypothalamus regulates many body processes that occur automatically. It also controls the pituitary gland.

The midbrain is below the middle of the forebrain. Its chief job is to manage the messages sent between the brain and spinal cord. Finally, the hindbrain sits below the back of the cerebrum. Part of it helps you balance and move.

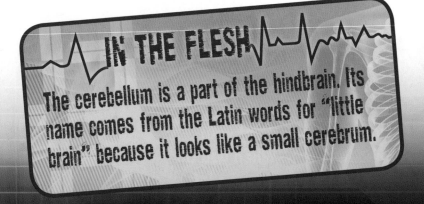

IN THE FLESH

The cerebellum is a part of the hindbrain. Its name comes from the Latin words for "little brain" because it looks like a small cerebrum.

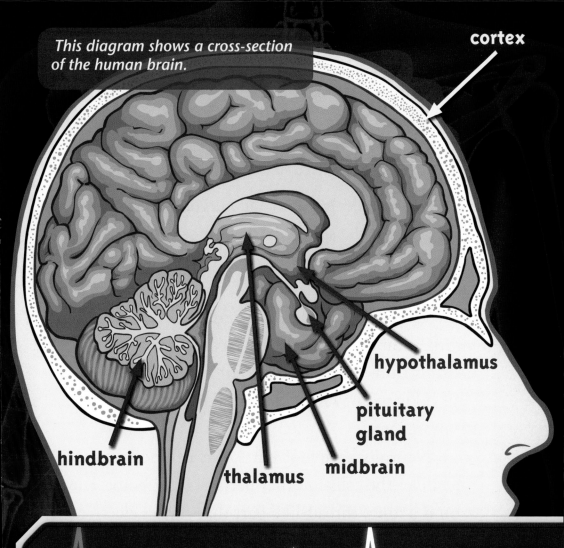

This diagram shows a cross-section of the human brain.

cortex

hindbrain

thalamus

midbrain

pituitary gland

hypothalamus

# BEHOLD THE BRAINSTEM

Together with the midbrain, parts of the hindbrain (called the pons and medulla) make up the brainstem. The brainstem's job is to receive, send out, and organize all the brain's messages. It's a little like the brain's secretary. It's also the part of the brain that helps with some of those actions that happen without any thought, like swallowing, blinking, breathing, and heartbeat.

# How It All Works

When talking about the nervous system, the brain and the spinal cord get most of the attention. But nerve cells, called neurons, are the real stars. When you see, smell, taste, and feel sticky strawberry jam, your sensory neurons hustle that information up to your brain right away. Motor neurons from the brain carry information telling your body to chew, swallow, and maybe even reach for more jam.

Neurons have four parts. The cell body is much like the cells in other parts of your body. The axon is a long, thread-like part that carries electrical impulses. The branched ends of axons, called axon terminals, send information to other neurons. Dendrites are branch-like parts that reach out toward other neurons to receive information.

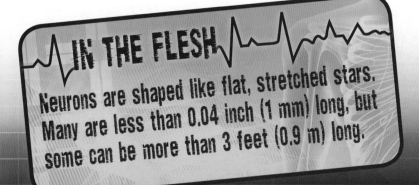

**IN THE FLESH**

Neurons are shaped like flat, stretched stars. Many are less than 0.04 inch (1 mm) long, but some can be more than 3 feet (0.9 m) long.

# THREE POUNDS AND 100 BILLION NEURONS

An adult brain only weighs about 3 pounds (1.4 kg), but it controls every single thing you do. With plenty of nooks and crannies, it has the extra surface area to save all the body's important information. Your brain contains more than 100 billion neurons, and they're so small you need a microscope to see them. Each one has a tiny axon and tiny dendrites reaching out to other neurons.

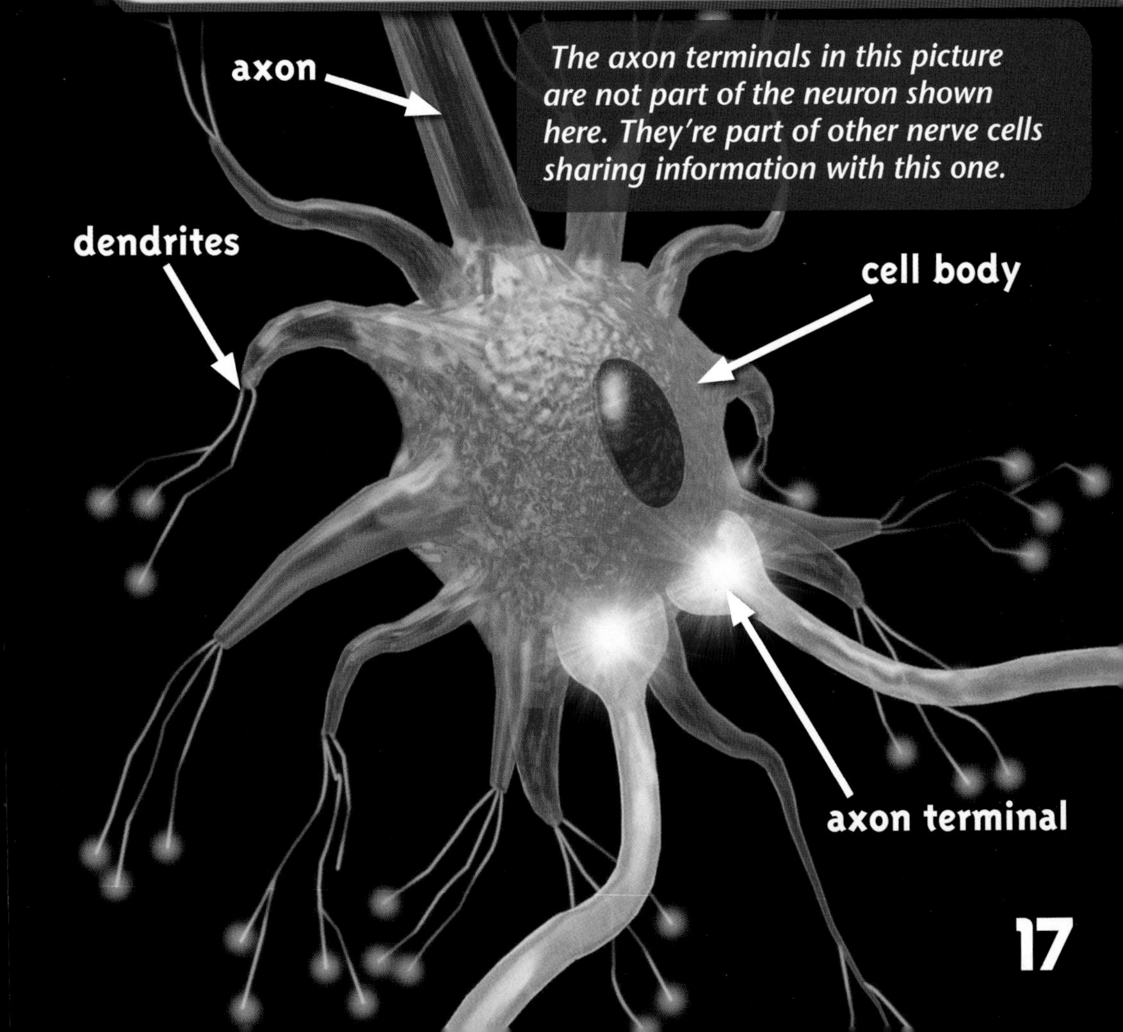

axon

*The axon terminals in this picture are not part of the neuron shown here. They're part of other nerve cells sharing information with this one.*

dendrites

cell body

axon terminal

Neurons in your nervous system are trading information all the time. One neuron may form contacts with 5,000 to 200,000 other neurons. These contacts are called synapses.

Neurons have two kinds of synapses. Electrical synapses, or gap junctions, are physical connections between the dendrites of different neurons. They allow electrical impulses to pass freely from one dendrite to another. Chemical synapses, or synaptic clefts, are spaces between the axon terminal of one neuron and the dendrite or cell body of another. When an electric signal reaches the axon terminal, the terminal releases a special chemical that crosses the synaptic cleft. The dendrite receives the chemical message, and turns it back into an electrical impulse. This pattern continues until the message reaches its destination.

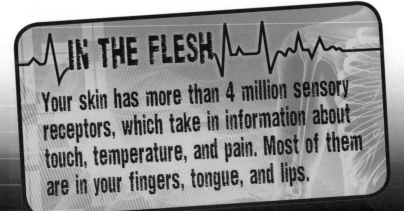

## IN THE FLESH

Your skin has more than 4 million sensory receptors, which take in information about touch, temperature, and pain. Most of them are in your fingers, tongue, and lips.

*This picture shows how chemical messengers cross the synaptic cleft between an axon terminal and a dendrite.*

axon terminal

synaptic cleft

dendrite

# LITTLE ALMONDS

Your brain is also in charge of your emotions, like when you're happy because you got a good grade or sad because you miss an aunt who lives far away. There are little clusters of cells on either side of your brain called amygdala (uh-MIHG-duh-luh). "Amygdala" means "almond," which is exactly what these clusters look like. Scientists think they control your emotions.

# Your Changing Brain

Did you know that your brain is changing all the time? You have billions of neurons that help you learn. As you learn more, the messages move between neurons over and over again. Once you do something enough, your brain notices patterns and creates pathways between the neurons to make things easier.

Think about how hard it can be to learn how to do something new, like swimming. At first, it can be really hard to remember how to move your arms and legs in the water, not to mention when to breathe without inhaling water. But don't give up. As you practice kicking and paddling more, your neurons send the same messages again and again. Eventually, your brain creates a "swimming" pathway, and soon you can swim!

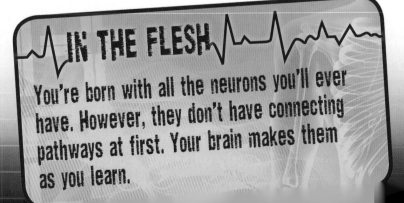

## IN THE FLESH

You're born with all the neurons you'll ever have. However, they don't have connecting pathways at first. Your brain makes them as you learn.

# BETTER BALANCE

The cerebellum is at the back of your brain. It's only a fraction of the size of the cerebrum, but it has a really important job to do. Balance, movement, and how your muscles work together—or coordination—are all controlled by your cerebellum. When you stand upright and walk around without toppling over, thank your cerebellum.

*Learning the motions required to so something—such as swimming—is often called muscle memory. The more you do something, the better your brain remembers how to move your muscles during that activity.*

# Diseases and Disorders

Unfortunately, things can go wrong with your body, and your nervous system is no exception. Doctors who help with nervous system **disorders** are called neurologists. Problems with the nervous system can show up as little changes in personality, more serious **symptoms** like blindness, or even death. Some disorders are **hereditary**, while others result from an **infection** or injury.

Infections can cause meningitis, which is an inflammation of the protective membranes of the brain and spinal cord. Shingles, or herpes zoster, can occur in someone who has been infected with the chicken pox virus. It attacks the nerve endings and causes a rash on the skin. Tetanus is a disorder caused by **bacteria** found in soil and manure. It attacks the nervous system and causes a tightening of the muscles.

## IN THE FLESH

Polio attacks motor neurons, but this disease has been almost completely eliminated across the world.

Ticks spread germs that cause neurological diseases. Lyme disease, for example, is spread by deer ticks.

# MULTIPLE SCLEROSIS

Multiple sclerosis (MS) cripples the central nervous system. It's called a demyelinating disease because it breaks down the **myelin sheath**. If the myelin sheath is damaged, nerve fibers can't work correctly. The **immune system** is often affected. Certain white blood cells attack the myelin as if it were an enemy. MS is the most common demyelinating disease, and its cause is unknown. Medications and physical therapy can help while scientists search for a cure.

# Brain in Shape!

You keep your body in shape with exercises such as running, swimming, and bike riding. You need to keep your brain and nervous system fit, too. How do you exercise your brain? There are lots of ways.

You should always eat a healthy diet with lots of food containing potassium and calcium. These minerals help your nervous system function properly. Go out and play! Exercise that's good for your body is also good for your nervous system. Always be sure to wear a helmet when you ride a bicycle or play any sport where you might bump your head. Avoid drinking alcohol, taking drugs, and smoking. Also, be sure to use your brain a lot by doing puzzles, reading books, and even painting or drawing.

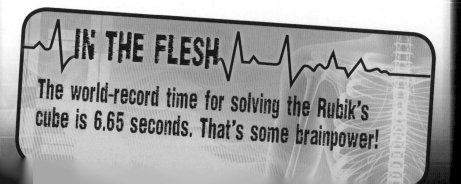

## IN THE FLESH

The world-record time for solving the Rubik's cube is 6.65 seconds. That's some brainpower!

# DO YOU SUDOKU?

If you really want to give your brain a tough workout to keep it in shape, try Sudoku. It's a number puzzle that uses three rows of three boxes. Some of the numbers are there, and you have to figure out the missing numbers. You could also try getting all the colored squares on one side of a Rubik's cube or even on all the sides! Other ideas are crossword puzzles and chess.

# Other Animals' Nervous Systems

Any animal that has a backbone has a nervous system similar to ours. Such animals are called vertebrates, and they include fish, birds, reptiles, amphibians, and other mammals. Generally, they have a brain and spinal cord that do a lot of the "heavy lifting." They also have a peripheral nervous system that carries messages between the brain and spinal cord and the rest of the body.

Invertebrates—animals that don't have a spinal cord—have different kinds of nervous systems. Many invertebrates have a nerve net, or a system of nerve cells and fibers that are distributed across the body like a net. For example, the jellyfish has a nerve net but no brain. The sponge doesn't have a clear-cut nervous system at all.

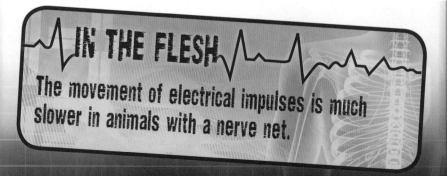

## IN THE FLESH

The movement of electrical impulses is much slower in animals with a nerve net.

# CORAL

It's hard to believe, but the coral animals you see in the sea have a nervous system, too! They don't have a brain, but they do have a basic nerve net. The net reaches from the coral's mouth to its tentacles. Some coral even have simple senses, like taste and smell.

These jellyfish are called sea nettles.

# Use Your Brain!

Life would be pretty dull without a nervous system. Without this complicated system of brain, spinal cord, and nerves, you couldn't whistle, draw, or play soccer. And what fun would that be? Your heart wouldn't beat and you couldn't breathe. Actually, you couldn't even exist!

It's easy to keep your nervous system in good working order. You might want to run out to school without eating, but listen to your parents when they tell you to have a healthy breakfast. Wearing a helmet when zipping around on your bicycle might seem uncool, but it will protect your head if you fall or get into an accident. Now that you know how much goes on in your noggin, don't you want to keep it safe?

# Your Noggin and Nervous System

- The pituitary gland is about the size of a pea.

- Electrical impulses in the nervous system are fast. Some travel faster than 200 miles (322 km) per hour!

- On average, an adult has about 0.5 cup (118 ml) of cerebrospinal fluid.

- For every square inch of surface area on your hand, you have 1,300 nerve endings.

- The sciatic nerves are the largest nerves in the human body. They contain the longest neurons in the body, which extend from the bottom of the spinal cord to the end of the big toes.

- Amnesia is a disorder caused by damage to the parts of the brain that store memories. It results in memory loss or the inability to form new memories.

- Scientists think that each of an octopus's eight arms has its own independent nervous system.

- A sperm whale's brain weighs about 17 pounds (7.8 kg). A green lizard's brain weighs just 0.003 ounce (0.08 g)!

# Glossary

**bacteria:** tiny creatures that can only be seen with a microscope

**cerebrospinal fluid:** a clear liquid that comes from the blood and helps cushion the brain and spinal cord

**disorder:** a physical or mental condition that is not normal

**gastrointestinal tract:** the system through which food moves and is broken down. The digestive system.

**gland:** organs in the body that make and release hormones

**hereditary:** passed from parent to child

**hormone:** a chemical made in the body that tells another part of the body how to function

**immune system:** the parts of the body that fight germs and keep it healthy

**infection:** the spread of germs inside the body, causing illness

**membrane:** a thin tissue in the body

**myelin sheath:** a protective layer around the axon of a nerve cell

**nerve:** a bundle of fibers that transmits messages in the body

**symptom:** something that suggests a disease or physical problem

**vertebrae:** the ring-shaped bones that make up the spine

# For More Information

## BOOKS

Jakab, Cheryl. *Nervous System*. North Mankato, MN: Smart Apple Media, 2006.

Macaulay, David. *The Way We Work: Getting to Know the Amazing Human Body*. Boston, MA: Houghton Mifflin, 2008.

Taylor-Butler, Christine. *The Nervous System*. New York, NY: Children's Press, 2008.

## WEBSITES

**Nervous System**
*yucky.discovery.com/noflash/body/pg000136.html*
Learn about the nervous system with this fun, short description.

**Neuroscience for Kids**
*faculty.washington.edu/chudler/nsdivide.html*
Check out facts, descriptions, and diagrams to learn more about the nervous system.

**Telegraph Line**
*www.schoolhouserock.tv/Telegraph.html*
This classic Schoolhouse Rock song teaches about the nervous system with fun song lyrics and a link to the video.

# Index

amnesia 29

amygdala 19

autonomic nervous system 8, 10

axon 16, 17

axon terminals 16, 17, 18, 19

brainstem 11, 15

cell body 16, 17, 18

central nervous system 6, 8, 10, 23

cerebellum 14, 21

cerebrospinal fluid 7, 29

cerebrum 12, 13, 14, 21

corpus callosum 12

cortex 14, 15

cranial nerves 10, 11

dendrites 16, 17, 18, 19

electrical impulses 16, 18, 26, 29

enteric nervous system 8

forebrain 12, 14

gap junctions 18

hemispheres 12, 13

hindbrain 12, 14, 15

hormones 10, 11

hypothalamus 10, 14, 15

invertebrates 26

lobes 12, 13

Lyme disease 23

membranes 7, 22

meninges 7

meningitis 22

midbrain 12, 14, 15

motor fibers 10, 16, 22

multiple sclerosis (MS) 23

myelin sheath 23

nerve net 26, 27

neurologists 22

neurons 16, 17, 18, 20, 29

parasympathetic nerves 8

pathways 20

peripheral nervous system 6, 8, 10, 26

pituitary gland 10, 11, 14, 15, 29

polio 22

sciatic nerves 29

sensory fibers 10, 16

shingles (herpes zoster) 22

spinal cord 4, 6, 7, 10, 14, 16, 22, 26, 28, 29

spinal nerves 10

sympathetic nerves 8, 9

synapses 18

synaptic clefts 18, 19

tetanus 22

thalamus 14, 15